T0166043

The Outsider's Guide to Your Veterans Benefits

By Michael Bushell

iUniverse, Inc.
New York   Bloomington

iUniverse books may be ordered through booksellers or by contacting:

iUniverse
1663 Liberty Drive
Bloomington, IN 47403
www.iuniverse.com
1-800-Authors (1-800-288-4677)

ISBN: 978-1-4401-1308-6 (sc)
ISBN: 978-1-4401-1309-3 (ebook)

Printed in the United States of America

iUniverse rev. date: 07/20/2009

Table of contents

Acknowledgements

I would like to give special thanks to Jackie D. Williams. Who have pushed me to do my best and staying positive through the process. Thanks to Tony D. Hardin for being a mentor and a friend. Thanks to Randall Johnson for believing in me and this book. Thanks to Kelly Walters-Smith, Jimmy Williams and Ms. Toya for editing my book. Thank you to my brothers and sisters in arms servicing in the military, retired from the military and the ones that gave their lives for my freedom.

Disclaimer

While all attempts have been made to verify information, in this publication neither the author nor the publisher assumes responsibility for our accuracy of our nation's actions or commitment to the cases of the subject matter herein. The author will uses the most common sir names to described or articulate the current subject matter. Please be advised that these are real cases, however, the real person's sir names was been changed. This book is intended to help veterans and their families receive benefits challenge the VA system. Attempting, to defraud the Federal government is practically impossible and/or will create more problems for you and your family. The Department of Veteran's Affairs will prosecute anyone to the fullest extent of the law if that person(s) is found defrauding the government.

All VA claims are subject to interpretation; this means similar claims can be interpreted differently by VA's claim raters. The claimant must be willing and able to fight for his is or her rights under U.S. Code Title 38.

The VA Outsider
Union City, GA 30291
Copyright © 2008 by Michael Bushell

Forward

In 1930, Congress established the Veterans Administration. Since its inception, the VA's record of accomplishment has been spotty at best and sordid at worst. Almost every U.S. Presidential candidate in the last sixty years (at least while campaigning) has acknowledged that the U.S. and particularly the Veterans Administration "needs to do better" by our nation's veterans. Yet, for most veterans, the handling of claims and benefits remains a nightmare of red tape, broken promises and immense frustration. In a book that is long overdue, Michael Bushell, a twenty-six year veteran of the regular Army and Army Reserves, and a disabled vet himself, has provided veterans with a plainspoken, common-sense guide to dealing with the VA in handling claims and benefits.

No one speaks the language of the veteran like another veteran---and no one speaks the lingo like Mike Bushell. He is not "just another veteran" but rather he is a vet who has lent his unique insight and intelligence to the task of researching some of the common problems that vets experience in trying to obtain the benefits promised to them by their country. As he says herein, "...after dealing with my own situation and doing research on the claims of other vets, we, as a country, are lucky that most people serve in the, military out a sense of duty, honor and patriotism.

Their service is not due to the benefits received or the promises kept by the VA to our veterans---the people who have truly saved the world for democracy."

It is sad that in this day of computers, artificial intelligence, the Internet, and other advanced technologies that such a book is needed. Nevertheless, needed, it is, as the VA has not improved its record of treating our veterans and their attendant issues. Thankfully, like the calvary in the days of horseback, Bushell has come thundering to the rescue. This is a book that should be read by every U.S. veteran and kept "right next to" his or her DD-214. A book should be owned and read by every American regardless of their veteran status.

Will Cantrell

June 2009

Chapter 1
Introduction

The journey from citizen to soldier to veteran is certainly full of ups and downs. In 2004, after spending more than twenty six years in the active Army and Reserves I retired and suddenly found myself immersed ------and overwhelmed------ in a system unlike anything that I had ever known. This 'system' is the Veterans Administration, better known as 'the VA'. In my transition from military life to civilian life, I quickly found that the use of the word 'system' when it comes to the VA was all wrong. More often than not, better terms to use would include "obstacle course", "web", "tangle", or even "mess". There are times when the word to use is unprintable.

The Department of Veterans' Affairs (or the VA) was originally created by Congress in order to assist veterans returning from military service to civilian life. Sad to say, many, many veterans, including the author, has encountered great difficulty in dealings with the VA. On too many occasions, I along with many other vets, found myself being talked down to, given misleading information, being mistreated by the gatekeepers of the system and denied services and rightful benefits. In spite of these issues, I learned with some patience, persistence and the use of the systems and procedures outlined in this book that you can receive all of your rightful benefits including the maximum amount of disability compensation.

This book will give you great insight as to how to get your VA benefits. The book will also help you to avoid misunderstandings, delays and especially frustration while applying for your VA benefits. It is critical that you **read** this information and **use** this knowledge to understand the VA system. Most importantly, the information contained in these pages contain a "STEP BY STEP" system that I have developed that will enable you to gain an edge in obtaining all of your VA benefits.

My Step BY Step System Works

About five months ago, I met Lieutenant Colonel (LTC) Jones in a gym on an Army base in Georgia five months ago. LTC Jones told me how the VA representative failed to give him basic information on how to file a claim or what to expect from the VA, or where to go for assistance and how long does the process take. LTC Jones told me "You have given me more information in fifteen minutes than the VA representative gave me in one hour. We continue to talk for another 15 minutes about my STEP X STEP system. If the VA is unwilling to help a LTC then how much help do you think an E-4 with traumatic brain injury will get from the VA. A few months passed, I saw LTC Jones again in gym. This time he was thanking me for all of my help. Because I clarified the process and he used the STEP BY STEP System outlined herein, found hidden information about filing his claim, LTC Jones received 90% disability rating on the first filing with the valuable knowledge he gained from me.

By using this book as a guide, you are not alone in the very often awkward transition from military life to civilian life. One of the key motivating factors for me in writing this book is due to Tony Hardin of the Veterans Resource Group (a nonprofit resource group that assists veterans and their families in their dealings with the VA) Tony challenged me to learn how the system works and help others by using the techniques that I learned. Understanding how the VA really works is vital to your long-term health and well being. To unlock the secrets of the VA benefits system; you must forget what you were told in the past, use this book as your guide and most importantly, be willing to fight for your rights!

Chapter 2
Remember when...

Think back for a moment to your separation briefing just before you left military service. If your briefing was anything like mine ------and that of most veterans----- the VA representative was nonchalant and halfhearted in explaining your rights and benefits as a veteran. You may have even been halfhearted in listening to the VA's rep because you were so happy to be leaving the military---maybe you were happy to just be alive.

Remember when the VA representative told your group "I am receiving 60% disability from the VA and I got my job because of my disability." *(Now, here the good part of the story.)* Remember when one of the soldiers, sailors, airmen or marines asked a simple but profound question. "So, how did you get 60%?" The VA representative started their song and dance routine and really didn't answer the question. The soldiers, sailors, airmen or marines may have unknowingly zeroed in on a key flaw with the VA and their intermediaries. The VA's organizational imperatives prevent them from giving you any information that maybe beneficial to you as it pertains to *filing a claim* with the VA. At the initial meeting the VA representative is trying to avoid the "informational minefield" in which someone can be

Michael Bushell

held accountable. However, the VA representative at
the same time is trying assist you transition from military
life to civilian/veteran life to make your transitional
period easier. Many transitioning vets do not check
the information being provided to them at this time.
Success will come after careful examination and
willingness to learn how the system work will prevent
major blunders in the future. There are several key
forms in your packet that are ***critical*** in choosing a
veterans service organization; the type of claim that
you are filing and the level of service that you may
require in the future. The forms include:

- VA form 21 –22 "Appointment of Veterans
  Service Organization as Claimant
  Representative"

- VA form 21 – 526 "Veterans Application for
  Compensation and/or Pension Part A B. C.
  and D"

- VA form 21 –0781 (Statement in Support of
  Claim for Service-Connected Post Traumatic
  Stress Disorder".

The VA representative gave these forms to you
however; he or she probably did not provide you with
a clear and concise way to complete the forms. VA
Form 21-0781(Statement In Support of Claim for
Service Connection for Post-Traumatic Stress Disorder

(PTSD)) will play an important part in your disability claim process if you served in Iraq or Afghanistan.

You are responsible for you and your family's wellbeing. Your VA representative's lack of commitment in answering questions because he or she is trying to add bodies to their rolls or must meet a quota of vets seen per day.

If this did not happen to you or this was not your experience with your first meeting then you are one of the lucky ones. However I heard countless tales on how the VA representative didn't give the vet any useful information to help them file their disability claims with VA. This is just one of the reasons why so many people believe that the VA has failed service members returning from the war. If you have a story of failure by the VA to meet your needs, you can contact me at www.vaoutsider@bellsouth.net

My surveys of unscientific however that does not mean the information gathered from my surveys is not valuable. My questions and the veterans' answers are very insightful and give you a vet's point of view about the VA.

Michael Bushell

**Survey of 1000 Veterans
Research provided by The Veterans Resource
Group**

How did they do it?

In May of 2007, I was waiting to see my VA representative. The waiting area was packed. There were veterans from WWII, Korea, Vietnam, Gulf War and the current wars. Many of the vets had been waiting for hours to be seen by their VA Representative. The mood became tense and the wait became more aggravating when one VA caseworker's relative---a veteran----was given special treatment by moving him ahead of the rest of the other vets. Yet, the VA will tell you "We do not have enough Vet Reps and that's why we cannot process your claim a timely manner." Or, "We treat everyone the same." You can believe that foolishness if you want to however the truth is people who work for the VA will take care of their family members and friend first before they will take care of you. In short, a small select group of vets have someone on the inside helping them while there is no one helping you.

This book will give you several strategies and techniques to better file for your VA disability claims. The sad truth is the VA has not changed the way they process compensation pension claims since World War II. The current system is unable to cope with the massive caseload already in the system and the new claims that are hitting the system every day. It is estimated that 3.4 million veterans, their dependents, widows and their parents are receiving some type of compensation from the VA. So where does it leave you? Your author has invested the time and effort to provide the reader with vital knowledge about the VA benefits process so you don't have to make the same mistakes or at least have the same challenges that have been faced in the beginning when I filed my claim. I've tackled the most difficult parts of the process and now here it is a simple STEP X STEP plan of attack for you to follow.

In the first step there are two parts, part one: Choosing a veterans' organization that will serve your goals and purposes. This step is a very important step because your service organization will be with you until the end of your life. I suggest <u>very strongly</u> that you do research on each service organization before choosing one. To help you make your choice, access <u>www.thevawatchdog.org</u> on the Internet. Here, you will find articles and surveys on the performance of the various service organizations that help veterans file for disability benefits. Part two: you will need your military medical and personnel records. Your medical and personnel records will enable you to accurately file your disability claim. It is suggested that you request everything in your medical and personnel records. Here's why. The majority of veterans filing for disability compensation doesn't remember or do not think that certain injuries are relevant or pertinent to their disability claims. I challenged this notion by asking Vets several questions: "Are you a doctor?" "Have you ever twisted your ankle or hurt your knee while doing physical training" and my last questions to them "Are you in pain now?" More often than not their answers never surprise me. They start remembering experiences and sometimes in graphic and painful detail. This is why it is <u>very important</u> that you use your medical and personnel records to file your VA claim. If you do not have your medical and personnel records then you can make a request to the National Personnel Records Center or ask your VA representative and to request that your records from Saint Louis, Missouri. They can contact them at:

National Personnel Records Center
Military Personnel Records
9700 Page Avenue
St. Louis, MO 63132-5100

You will need to complete a Standard Form 180 to receive your records. Note that this process can take up to 24 months to complete. (For this reason, it is advisable to obtain these records for safekeeping <u>immediately after exiting the service.)</u>

Here's one vets sad story: I met Mr. Johnson in front of the VA hospital and we were talking about VA benefits. Mr. Johnson works for the United States Post Office. He told me many of his co-workers at the Post Office are receiving VA benefits up to 100% in some cases. However Mr. Johnson is one of those unfortunate vets that does not have strong contacts

Michael Bushell

within the VA system and did not have his medical and personnel records. After the first time he was denied an increase in benefits, received a rating of 10%. He became discouraged. Mr. Johnson asked me "Why did this happen to him?" while he did not understand how people at the Post Office with similar disabilities received much higher rating. It was apparent that Mr. Johnson was very frustrated and discontented with the whole process. The sad truth is no one at the Post Office could help Mr. Johnson with the basic information on where to get his medical and personnel records. Everyone, from his VA representative to his coworkers gave Mr. Johnson half hearted attempts and disinformation. He may receive some type of benefit increase however there will be a long time coming and may not reflect his seriousness of his disabilities. Part of Mr. Johnson problem was he did not take matters into his own hands and managed the process. He only relied on the VA to help him…big mistake. Mr. Johnson did not work the system. He should have never taken no for a finally answer. He did not do the basic research about how the process work, Although cronyism and nepotism runs rampant within the VA system you can avoid this from happening to you must be diligent and the steadfast throughout this whole process. I never saw Mr. Johnson again. I truly hope that Mr. Johnson received the benefits that he deservers. For more information about your VA benefits go to www. vaoutsider@bellsouth.net

Does Cronyism And Nepotism Run Rampant Within the VA?

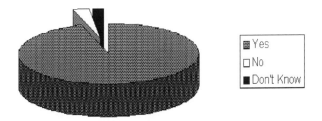

Yes
No
Don't Know

Survey of 1000 Veterans
Research provided by The Veterans Resource Group

Chapter 3
How does the system work?

Many veterans ask "How does the VA system work" To give an honest answer the system doesn't work. Since the 1950's, the Department of Veterans Affairs and the Congress knew of serious problems with filing claims for disability and pension. They failed to solve a growing problem yet the Department of Veterans Affairs and the Congress have reduced or eliminated many needed programs and options for veterans to put their lives back together again after the trauma of war. These are not the ramblings of a disgruntled veteran but the findings of the Office of The Inspector General within the VA. "The commission concluded that the situation was not a recent development, but had existed at least four decades cited as an example a study of rooted in the nineteen fifties which reach an accord that concluded the VA's analysis of legislature and other problems showed a noticeable lack of basic factual data."1 Also in this report, the Office of The Inspector General points out five major problems with the VA and the way it processes disability claims. The five major areas are: 1. ineffective planning, 2. incoherent implementation, 3. inadequate review and analysis of program performance data 4. executive staff not being held accountable for performance improvements, 5, reliance on after the fact, controls over quality rather than building it in at the beginning of the adjudication process. 2 Coupled with these ongoing problems within The Department of Veterans Affairs, they use your best qualities against you. They know that your discipline and loyalty to the government will hinder you from seeking the truth. The major service organizations and the VA's staff fail to inform us about our rights and what can be expected from the VA. There are claims that the VA has gotten better, however, the facts remain that claims-processing and lack of information about individual claims still persists. It is your obligation to find out... how the VA works or doesn't work so that you can be prepared to meet the challenges of dealing with the VA. I tested these no-nonsense steps on my claim and my results were dramatic. I maximized my rating from 60% to 90% within 2 years. I know many veterans personally that after 10 years of receiving disability benefit they are only receiving the minimum amount.

Here is a perfect example of what I am talking about. One day I spoke to a Master Sergeant Smith about his claim with the VA. Master Sergeant Smith had part of his lung removed, knee surgery and nerve damage in his lower back. Based on the VA's rules, Master Sergeant Smith should have received over 90% disability rating or higher. Unfortunately, Master Sergeant Smith only received 30% disability rating. He could not believe his rating was so low. I asked Master Sergeant Smith several questions. "One, did you complete your own packet?" Master Sergeant Smith said no. "Two, did you push yourself although you were in pain when the doctor asked you to touch your toes, bend your knees and run on the treadmill?" Master Sergeant Smith answered yes, I did. My final question to him was "If you were in so much pain why didn't you say so or why didn't you stop?" He looked puzzled and answered because ***I wanted to do my best***. I said to him, "Your best only got 30%." You must take a long-term view of your situation. Although he completed the paperwork correctly and had proper documentation showing his disabilities, he failed to follow my advice. To manage and control the parts of the process that is in your hands. Master Sergeant Smith assumed doing his best well get him more. In the end, it had the opposite effect on his disability rating. The Department of Veterans Affairs wants you to go away, once you not to file or just die. So they don't have to pay your disability coverage for the remainder of your life because it's cheaper in the long run for the VA. Form VBA 21-526 is the other way the VA tries to discourage you from your claim. This form is extremely long and confusing. However, this is the only way for you to apply for your benefits. You must be organized and have all your documentation or have someone to assist if you are unable to complete the form. Organization is the key to success. (A copy of VBA 21-526 is a the end of the chapter)

Within the next three years, the VA will receive over 875,000 new claims for disability. The question is

Michael Bushell

"Where do you fit in?" If you do not want to end up like Master Sergeant Smith you should do the following:

1. Complete VBA 21 –526 yourself by using your medical and personnel records.

2. Complete VA Form 21-4138 yourself by using your medical and personnel records for change in status.

3. List all injuries, illnesses, treatments prescribed by the doctor and/or changes to medication.

4. Use the " who, what, where and how method of describing your injuries illnesses and treatments

5. Do your homework or your injuries, illnesses the treatments recommended by your doctor

6. Keep all of your doctor's appointments

At the beginning of this book, I pointed out several things that you must do. The first step had two parts to it. Choosing a service organization that works for you is very important. This service organization will represent you until the end of your life. You must choose wisely. You must have your medical records to get started. Without your medical and personnel records you are at the mercy of the VA. (See illustration 1) The illustration shows what, when, who and where. This method is the simplest and most straight foreword method because there is one to one match between the incident and the treatment for both forms. It gives you better opportunity clearly pinpoint your injuries and illnesses on VA Form 21-438. VA Form 21-438 is to update an existing claim and used as a supplemental information sheet (see illustration 2) in illustration 2, the veteran is seeking an increase in his disability rating. His current health problems are now becoming chronic due his experiences in Kuwait while serving at the port. Listed below are several key phases that will highlight and pinpoint your claim.

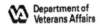 **Department of Veterans Affairs**

VA Form 21-526, Part B: Compensation

Use this form to apply for compensation. Remember that you must also fill out a VA Form 21-526, Part A: General Information, for your application to be processed. Be sure to write your name and Social Security number in the space provided on page 2.

SECTION I	Tell us about your disability	In the table below, tell us more about your disability or disabilities. Be sure to: • List all disabilities you believe are related to military service • List all the treatments you received for your disabilities, including • treatments you received in a military facility before and after discharge. • treatments you received from civilian and VA sources before, during, and after your service.

1. What disability are you claiming?	2. When did your disability begin?	3. When were you treated?	4a. What medical facility or doctor treated you?	4b. What is the address of that medical facility or doctor?
Lower Back Pain	11/01/1999 *mo day yr*	*from* 11/01/1999 *mo day yr* / *to* 12/31/2006 *mo day yr*	Maj. Brown, LTC Jones, Dr. Yang, Cpt. Smith-Young, Dr. Quick	The Clinics at: Ft. Gordon, Ft. Bragg, Ft. Drum and Ft. Benning
Broken Right and Left legs	06/09/2000 *mo day yr*	*from* 06/09/2000 *mo day yr* / *to* 11/21/2000 *mo day yr*	LTC Jones	Ft. Bragg
Shot in Left Shoulder	02/27/2003 *mo day yr*	*from* 02/27/2003 *mo day yr* / *to* 05/10/2003 *mo day yr*	Col. Thomas	Landstuhl Germany
		from / *to*		

Michael Bushell

VA Department of Veterans Affairs	STATEMENT IN SUPPORT OF CLAIM

PRIVACY ACT INFORMATION: The VA will not disclose information collected on this form to any source other than what has been authorized under the Privacy Act of 1974 or Title 38, Code of Federal Regulations 1.576 for routine uses (i.e., civil or criminal law enforcement, congressional communications, epidemiological or research studies, the collection of money owed to the United States, litigation in which the United States is a party or has an interest, the administration of VA Programs and delivery of VA benefits, verification of identity and status, and personnel administration) as identified in the VA system of records, 58VA21/22, Compensation, Pension, Education and Rehabilitation Records - VA, published in the Federal Register. Your obligation to respond is required to obtain or retain benefits. VA uses your SSN to identify your claim file. Providing your SSN will help ensure that your records are properly associated with your claim file. Giving us your SSN account information is voluntary. Refusal to provide your SSN by itself will not result in the denial of benefits. The VA will not deny an individual benefits for refusing to provide his or her SSN unless the disclosure of the SSN is required by Federal Statute of law in effect prior to January 1, 1975, and still in effect. The requested information is considered relevant and necessary to determine maximum benefits under the law. The responses you submit are considered confidential (38 U.S.C. 5701). Information submitted is subject to verification through computer matching programs with other agencies.

RESPONDENT BURDEN: We need this information to obtain evidence in support of your claim for benefits (38 U.S.C. 501(a) and (b)), Title 38, United States Code, allows us to ask for this information. We estimate that you will need an average of 15 minutes to review the instructions, find the information, and complete this form. VA cannot conduct or sponsor a collection of information unless a valid OMB control number is displayed. You are not required to respond to a collection of information if this number is not displayed. Valid OMB control numbers can be located on the OMB Internet Page at www.whitehouse.gov/omb/library/OMBINV.html#VA If desired, you can call 1-800-827-1000 to get information on where to send comments or suggestions about this form.

FIRST NAME - MIDDLE NAME - LAST NAME OF VETERAN (Type or print) Johnston, Mickey L.	SOCIAL SECURITY NO. XXX XX 1213	VA FILE NO. C/CSS -XXX XX 12

The following statement is made in connection with a claim for benefits in the case of the above-named veteran:

While serving and living on the Port of Kuwait during the periods of 12/01/2002 to 04/24/2004. I was exposed to

ammonia releases 24 times within a 14 month period. I experienced shorten of breath, fatigue and sharp pains

in chest. The medic at the clinic prescribed an inhaler treatments for several months. My wife has woke me up

several times during my sleep because of my snoring.

ILLUSTRATION 2

As I mentioned previous chapters, you must do your homework and understand your illness, treatment, symptoms and disease. Within your explanation, you should include key words: chronic, acute, intense, prolong, aggravated and persistent. These words are used by physicians to describe their patients' condition. By using these words, you also indicate to everyone that you're serious about understanding and managing your disabilities. You must present your case in a concise, well written manner because the VA staffer reviewing your claim will likely not try to figure out what you mean or are trying to say. A clear, well written document will keep you ahead of the game. Please remember it is your responsibility to manage the process. Focusing on the basic rules within this book and taking charge of the process (i.e. not haphazardly leaving it in the hands of the VA and waiting for them to call you will improve your chances of receiving maximum disability claim on the first attempt.

The real deal with your VA Representative

A close friend told me a story about people at her job. My friend is an administer for a nursing facility in Georgia. She said 20% of my staff always does their best for the patients, their families and the facility. "However 80% won't do a damn thing and they're here just to collect a check." I suspect that these words are true for many organizations, including the VA. You'll find your VA representative and the Service Organizations' Representative are cut from the same cloth. Recently, I had a conversation with a service organization representative. He tried to convince me that he was working on my behalf. I asked him a simple question that seemed to irritate him. I asked **"What is the purpose of your organization and how does it benefit me?"** He sat up in his chair and said "We help you file your claim for disability and represent you in any appeals with the VA." I told him I filed my own claim and the first time I receive 60% disability without the help of your organization. The second time I sought a re-evaluation and I received 80%. I'm not sure if I need you or your organization to represent me. He quickly tried to turn the conversation to something else but I would not let it go. His organization could not help me file a vocational rehabilitation claim for retraining and

23

Michael Bushell

educational benefits something that I really needed. Once again, I asked "why do I need your help and you can't help me file for vocational rehabilitation training?"

Let me stop here and tell you what the real point is. Most of these people can't help themselves in filing their own this disability claims. So, the real question is, "How can they help you?" These groups are part of the system and they will only do what is in the best interest for the VA. You will do a lot of the work yourself. Hopefully, you will find the twenty percenters that are willing and able to assist you in filing your VA disability claim. This person will be competent, highly qualified and willing to go the extra mile for you. However, more than likely you will get one of the eighty percenters whose real job is to collect papers and pass it to someone else without rechecking it or verified the contents.

The former Health and Human Services Secretary, Dr. Donna Shalala, said this about the VA's disability rating system. "The whole disability rating system is broken and needs to be changed."3 Their actions are only hurting the veteran in the long run. The sad truth is these are our fellow veterans not looking out for other veterans or worst, a civilian with no clue of your service to the nation. Just last year National Public Radio's Ari Shapiro investigated allegations that the US Army asked the Department of Veterans Affairs to stop helping injured soldiers complete their Army disability paperwork. The VA said OK! 4 At this point, do you still feel that I am a bitter veteran? To void any major problems with filing your disability claim, you must do careful and comprehensive research on the group that will assist you with your new challenges ahead.

Chapter 4
The facts and nothing but the facts

Providing clear and concise about you information about your disabilities may make the process of filing a little bit faster. There are several ways to filing your claims; however, **the most effective way is listing your problems in chronological order from your medical and personnel records**. It is very important that you start from the beginning and end at the present or just before you were discharged from military service. Because of the VA's archaic system, you need to increase your odds of success by clearly presenting your information to the VA. This is not a guarantee the VA will do the right thing. On many occasions, veterans presented a clear and concise roadmap of their disabilities for the VA. Just to have the VA deny the disability claims or award the veteran the lowest rating for their disabilities. The rating specialists at the VA are supposed to be competent, fair and objective. In many instances, this is not the case. Here is an example of the subjective bias of a ratings specialist. Subjective bias is very difficult to overcome because of the random nature of this emotion. Yes, I said emotion. The VA would have you to believe that all decisions are made in a sterile environment free from emotion. I am here to tell you this is not the case.

The factors for subjective bias in the claim rating process are too numerous to mention. However, gross incompetence, sexism, racism; misgivings on the outcome of previous and/or current wars are some of the factors I've found in subjective bias. By uncovering the secrets of Title 38 Pensions, Bonuses, and Veterans' Relief, I learned vital information that has gotten positive result in the pass. Title 38 is the secret that you're not told about because it will help you in filing your disability benefit claims. Please remember the rules are set up to protect the VA however there's enough information in Title 38 to give you a fighting chance to reduce the level of subjective biases. Just like anything else in the government, this information is not user friendly. Under Title 38 there are several parts that I recommend researched before you file your claim. These parts are as follows: *3 – Adjudication, 4 – Schedule for Rating Disabilities, 10 – Adjust Compensation 17 – Medical, 19 – Board of Veterans' Appeals: Appeal Regulations and 20 - Board of Veterans' Appeals: Rules of Practice.* These sections will help you file the best claim that you can file or assist you in preparing a strong appeal against the VA.

Subjective biases are the key tactics used by the VA to deny what is rightfully yours. The information I am giving you now was too late for Mr. Jefferson to use in developing a better plan of attack against the VA. Just last week I met with a real American hero. Mr. Jefferson served with distinction in Vietnam during the mid sixties to the mid eighties. He made over 28 parachute jumps into Vietnam. He has fought the Viet Cong and parts of the Red Army and has received several Purple Hearts. He is one of few Marines that received the Air Force Flight Medal. He is a true patriot. However, the VA has denied his disability claim on dubious grounds. Looking through his paperwork, I was very impressed with the level of detail and accuracy that he laid out about his disabilities. Mr. Jefferson was clearly upset and disappointed that his disability claim was denied by the VA. The U.S. Navy and the Department of Veterans Affairs knows of Mr. Jefferson's experience in Vietnam as well the rest of his military career. They are trying to save themselves from embarrassment due to the fact that Mr. Jefferson has them dead to rights because someone at the VA failed to do their job. The VA says Mr. Jefferson is permanently and totally disabled but not from his military service. We both commented that the ratings specialists clearly failed in interpreting Mr Jefferson's claim. This happened to a highly disciplined and decorated Vietnam veteran to twenty years of service in the military. I shudder to think what would happen to a poor kid with a traumatic brain injury with only a high school diploma and no real help from the VA.

It is this kind of subjective bias and gross incompetence that raises the ire of veterans over the handling of their disability claims. Clearly, some one felt Mr. Jefferson did not deserve fair treatment under Title 38. Two thirds of all veterans feel that the VA shows some type of bias. Currently, there are 3.5 million vets, dependent children, widows and parents of deceased servicemembers receiving compensation from the VA. If you really break it down, this means there are over 2 million customers dissatisfied with the VA (or the entire population of the city of Minneapolis). It is our right as Americans to have a system that works for us and not work against us. Veterans blame this debacle of a system on the political leaders (of both political parties); every three months it seems they're doing something on veterans' rights and fail to do anything of real importance in the lives of veterans. Our leaders seem unable or unwilling to fix the problems at the VA. The Republicans and Democrats are equally guilty in their blatant lack of will power to solve this crisis. If Social Security is the greatest challenge to the American socio-economic responsibility in the late 20th century then veteran's rights and disability compensation are the new fault line of the 21st century. We are witnessing a new wave of homelessness, poverty, mental illness from people who have served their country valiantly and with honor. This disaster is unprecedented in the annals of American history.

This is why it is your right to seek out information and make sure you do your homework. The application of the knowledge that I'm giving you may prevent your anger and frustration with the VA in the long run.

For more information about your VA benefits go to www.vaoutsider@bellsouth.net

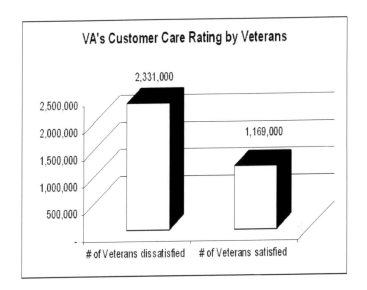

Research provided by the Veterans Resource Group

Chapter 5
Wait and see

What really happens when veterans file their claims? This seems to be one of the greatest mysteries throughout the whole process. The Office of the Inspector General said the following about claim processing timeliness: "The length of time required for the VA to process claims (and in particular compensation claims) needs to be reduced. Veterans applying for their first (i.e. original) claim monthly compensation based on an injury or illness resulting from their military service can expect to wait over eight months for the VA to approve or disapprove the claim – about twice as long as the Veterans Benefits Administration's (VBA) goal and about four times longer than veterans expect. Further, veterans applying for an increase that is already approved for existing claim (85% of all compensation applications) will wait a similar amount of time (four months). In most cases an appeal by veterans of a VA decision will extend the wait on average to 36 months to 52 months – ahead to an average of three years or less as recently as the late nineteen nineties. Although these time frames would suggest that compensation claims are extremely complex, on average the processing time for a compensation claim requires only 7 hours of actual hands on work by the

VA's employees, with the remaining time spent waiting for information or floating in neverland."5 What does is really mean? Let me break it down for you. From start to finish, a veteran's claim for compensation will take over 540 days to 705 days waiting to be processed. However it takes only 7 hours to 24 hours of actual processing time on a veteran's claim. The Inspector General's Office did not take into account the volume of new claims coming into the system on top of the backlog. These ridiculously long processing time places undue stress upon the injured veteran and their families causing catastrophic consequences within a veteran's family structure. Homelessness, joblessness, abnormally high suicide rates and abnormally high divorce rates are the primarily symptoms of the VA's lack of commitment to veterans and their families. This is an outrage and very hypocritical of our leadership in America. They are willing to send men and women to fight for America but won't help them in a timely manner when they return.

If you were upset about that, the appeals process is even worse. A denied claim may take as long as four and a half years to be adjudicated by the VA. This is a classic stall tactic by the VA to not pay veterans their compensation. This is why many veterans feel the VA is waiting for them to die so the VA can pay less money in the long run. To add insult to injury, the Office of The Inspector General said about the quality of claims adjudication decisions. "The most frequently cited evidence that the quality of claim adjudication is inadequate is highest rate with which appeal cases (90% of which are compensation cases) are remanded (sent back) by the Board of Veterans' Appeals (BVA) to the originating VA Regional Office (RO) for additional information or reconsideration. Currently about half of all appeal cases are remanded – which can and add additional two years to the veterans wait for a decision on their benefit claim. The high remand rate, combined with BVA ruling in favor in veterans and 20% of the appeal cases plus another 10% of appealed cases reversed by the ROs themselves on remand, is interpreted by Veteran's Service Organizations VSO's (which represents veterans before BVA) as proof that the ROs are not properly adjudicating veterans claims."6 The Department of Veterans Affairs lack of action is unacceptable. If the shoe was on the other foot, your congressman or senator would be leading protest marches down Pennsylvania Avenue. The real question is "Do they really care about veterans and veterans' rights?" and "When are they going to fix the problem?"

Last year I worked with Sergeant Thomas. She had several major problems when she returned from Iraq. I help her to organize her paperwork and I explained the process to her. The war deeply affected her in such a profound way that she can hardly function on a day to day basis.

We started her paperwork in May of 2006 however she did not get an answer until the end of December of 2007. Somewhere in between this time, Sergeant

Michael Bushell

Thomas was forced into bankruptcy. She lost her house, car and her marriage. She will call me periodically and ask this one question "Why does it take long?" I sat quietly for a few minutes before I gave my answer to her. I said "I don't know!" The fact of the matter is; there is no answer to justify any delay of paying her benefits. There are parts of the process where the VA is unable to tell you in any definite terms who has your paperwork and where is it within the processing pipeline. Is it being mailed from one regional office to another? Is it sitting on some clerk's desk? Is it at the rating board? Nobody knows and it seems like nobody cares. This affects all of us who have filed of VA claims and shows a blatant disrespect for veterans and their families. Not only is the VA wasting time and money by back paying everyone in the system because they are unable or unwilling to solve this problem. My only recommendations are to make duplicate copies of your paperwork before submitting it to the VA, make all your doctor's appointments and be patient and diligent in waiting for your claim to be process. Unfortunately this process is out of your hand.

Chart of Claims Adjudication/Approval Process
(Typical Original Compensation Claims)

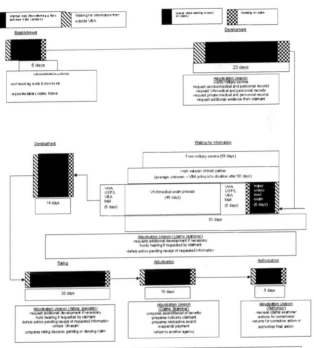

You may and notice that my time frame is higher than the inspector general because I calculated in two key factors. Factors are backlog claims to be filed and employees leave the system.

Chapter 6
The doctor will see you now

After you completed all your forms, attended endless meetings with your VA rep and waited by your mailbox for any sign of life from the VA. You will receive a letter to mail me giving you instructions on making your next step in the your claim process. Your Total Quality Care (TQC) appointment letter will advise you on several things. The letter has several parts. The first part will give you the name and location of your doctor and the second part will inform you the type of evaluation that you are scheduled for. This is where the veteran's disciple and training is used against him or her to limit or to deny their benefit claims. It is imperative that you research and understand the disability that you are applying for. I am not telling you however to lie or falsify any information that you provide to your doctor, VA rep or to the Federal Government. These actions will have serious consequences and should not be done under any circumstance. However, it is clearly spelled out under Title 38 the symptoms, injuries and ailments that you may have claimed on your disability compensation form. Understanding what you're asking for and knowing something about your symptoms, injuries and illness will help you effectively communicate with your doctor. Most vets do not take the time to do this. They are still under the impression that the system is about justice and fairness and become very disillusioned when they do not get the results that they seek.

Sergeant Kahn did his homework and researched his disability. He suffered from severe sleep apnea. He conveyed to me several times during the night his wife would have to wake him up because he had stopped breathing. This clearly was affecting his quality of life. He was unable to sleep, which in turn created several problems for him at work and in his personal relationships. The military was forcing him out due to the problems that he was having. I asked him had the military doctors performed a sleep study to determine the level of his sleep apnea. He said no. I recommend to Sgt. Kahn to request a sleep study from the military. He had 60 days before he was to be separated from the military and I convinced him it was imperative that he have the sleep study done as soon as possible and submit his information directly to the VA. Sergeant Kahn followed by my instructions and within eight months received 50% disability for sleep apnea.

On the other hand Master Sergeant Roberts did not listen and received only 30% disability for injuries, illnesses or ailments that should have been rated way higher. Master Sergeant Robert had several operations on his foot, lung damage from the first Gulf War and severe hearing loss. This is where the VA doctors used Master Sergeant Roberts' training against him. Master

Sergeant Roberts was a high speed, low drag soldier. He did everything that he was told to do no matter how painful or uncomfortable it was to him. When the doctor asked Master Sergeant Roberts "How are you going today?" he replied I'm doing fantastic. This started his downward spiral because he tried to do his best and he still thought that he was a high speed dedicated motivated soldier. He pushed pass his pain and performed all tasks like the high speed soldier that he was. He felt good about evaluation he said. Little did he know he had sabotage his own disability evaluation. Please remember the evaluation starts from the time you walk into the door until you walk out the door. Managing this part of the processes is key to receiving the rating that truly reflects your disabilities. My recommendation is very simple, be open and honest about your pain, your injury, your illness and your symptoms.

Too many times soldiers, sailors, airmen and marines have these to prove to themselves and to the doctors that they're not hurt or that their are tough. There's no shame in admitting that you gave your own for your country with your brothers and sisters in arms. You must dig into Title 38 part 4.17 and understand how the doctor's rating system works. The Internet has made researching for your benefit easier by having The US Codes of Federal Regulations or CFRs. (http://ecfr. gpoaccess.gov) The evidence is there. If you word your claim with the correct terms, have the medical documentation to support the facts and researched

Michael Bushell

Title 38 to seek a clear understanding of your medical problems, there is a strong possibility that you will improve your chances on receiving a rating over 20% or more. Like all aspects of your life you must manage this process to receive the maximum benefit, if not, you are just wasting your time.

Department of Veterans Affairs	STATEMENT IN SUPPORT OF CLAIM

PRIVACY ACT INFORMATION: The VA will not disclose information collected on this form to any source other than what has been authorized under the Privacy Act of 1974 or Title 38, Code of Federal Regulations 1.576 for routine uses (i.e., civil or criminal law enforcement, congressional communications, epidemiological or research studies, the collection of money owed to the United States, litigation in which the United States is a party or has an interest, the administration of VA Programs and delivery of VA benefits, verification of identity and status, and personnel administration) to identified in the VA system of records, 58VA21.22, Compensation, Pension, Education and Rehabilitation Records - VA, published in the Federal Register. Your obligation to respond is required to obtain or retain benefits. VA uses your SSN to identify your claim file. Providing your SSN will help ensure that your records are properly associated with your claim file. Giving us your SSN account information is voluntary. Refusal to provide your SSN by itself will not result in the denial of benefits. The VA will not deny an individual benefits for refusing to provide his or her SSN unless the disclosure of the SSN is required by Federal Statute of law in effect prior to January 1, 1975, and still in effect. The requested information is considered relevant and necessary to determine maximum benefits under the law. The responses you submit are considered confidential (38 U.S.C. 5701). Information submitted is subject to verification through computer matching programs with other agencies.

RESPONDENT BURDEN: We need this information to obtain evidence in support of your claim for benefits (38 U.S.C. 501(a) and (b)). Title 38, United States Code, allows us to ask for this information. We estimate that you will need an average of 15 minutes to review the instructions, find the information and complete this form. VA cannot conduct or sponsor a collection of information unless a valid OMB control number is displayed. You are not required to respond to a collection of information if this number is not displayed. Valid OMB control numbers can be located on the OMB Internet Page at www.whitehouse.gov/omb/library/OMBINV.html#VA. If desired, you can call 1-800-827-1000 to get information on where to send comments or suggestions about this form.

FIRST NAME - MIDDLE NAME - LAST NAME OF VETERAN (Type or print)	SOCIAL SECURITY NO.	VA FILE NO.
Ali Jaru Kahn	XXX-XX-9039	C/CSS - XXXXX9039

The following statement is made in connection with a claim for benefits in the case of the above-named veteran:

During my serve in Iraq 4/2003 to 11/2004, I had problems sleeping and breathing at night. The soldiers in my

tent made a request to the Sergeant Major of the battalion have me move out of the tent. The field hospital

diagnosis me with sleep apnea however was unable to properly treat me during to a lack equipment or the

severity of my illness. Take effected my job performance and my professional relationships. My wife forced me

to go to the Army Hospital get treatment because it was ruining our relationship at home. When I returned to

the States, the Army Hospital on post issued me a breathing machine that I wear nightly.

ILLUSTRATION 3

Chapter 7
50%+20%+20%+10%+10%+0%=70%

OK, you have made it through all the craziness. You got an award letter in the mail saying "Dear Mr. Jones: We have made a decision on your claim for service-connected compensation received on June 1 2004. This tells details you about your entitlement amount and payment start date and what we decided. It includes a copy of your rating decision that gives the evidence and reason for our decision. We also included information about additional benefits, what to do if you disagree with our decision and who to contact if you have any questions or need assistance." You're getting excited because you reached the end of the line. All your hard work, pain and suffering have paid off. So you flip through your paperwork and you notice the percentages don't add up. For example you may receive 50% for post traumatic stress disorder, 20% for degenerative disc disease, 20% for fibroid tumors, 10% for irritable bowl disorder, 10% for plataritas and other foot problems and 0% nerve damage in right hand. In fifth grade, adding 50% plus 20% plus 20% plus 10% plus 10% plus 0% equals 110%. However, in the Orwellian world of the VA this only equal 70%. The VA is nickeling and dimeing veterans to death with this outmoded and outlandish rating system. This is how it

Michael Bushell

really works. Here is the VA's explanation: **Higher of two evaluations.**

"*Where there is a question as to which of two evaluations shall be applied, the higher evaluation will be assigned if the disability picture more nearly approximates the criteria required for that rating. Otherwise, the lower rating will be assigned.*"**7**

The VA will take the greatest percentage of your disability and take portions of the remaining of the percentages to create a combined overall rating. This new math plus the ridiculously long processing period is cruel treatment that national hero should not endure. Cheating the very same people who defend our country is disgraceful, shameless and criminal. We must demand better treatment and better care of our living national treasures. You must be prepared to stand your ground and demand better treatment and a more equitable system for all. The best way to stand your ground in these cases is to prepare your paperwork yourself, and seek outside medical treatments/opinions. An outside Physician is not beholden to the VA and will provide none bias and objective perspective on your health. However, there are large numbers of veterans may not have the option of outside medical consultation. There are volunteer groups around the nation will help you file your claims.

The following groups may provide some assistance in completing the disability paperwork:

Wounded Warriors
National Military Family Association
Fisher House Foundation
In the Metro Atlanta Area:
The Veterans Resource Group

When you talk to your VA representative, you should have a clear game plan on what you're trying to accomplish by filing your disability claim. In the next section, you have two options if you are dissatisfied with your disability rating. I clearly explain both the risks and the rewards of each course of actions.

Sometimes the hardest rating to change is a rating of 10% and the easiest rating to charge is a 0% rating. Once again VA's new math and Orwellian logic can frustrate the best of us. You must focus on the goal and not give to their madness.

Michael Bushell

Veterans Compensation Benefits Rate Tables - Effective 12/1/07

Basic Rates - 10%-100% Combined Degree Only

Rates (No Dependents): 10% - 20%

Without Children	With Children
30% - 60%	30% - 60%
70% - 100%	70% - 100%

To find out how to use these rate tables CLICK HERE

10% - 20% (No Dependents)

Percentage	Rate
10%	$117
20%	$230

30% - 60% without Children

Veteran Alone	$356	$512	$728	$921
Veteran with Spouse Only	$398	$568	$799	$1006
Veteran with Spouse & One Parent	$432	$613	$856	$1074
Veteran with Spouse and Two Parents	$466	$658	$913	$1142
Veteran with One Parent	$390	$557	$785	$989
Veteran with Two Parents	$424	$602	$842	$1057
Additional for A/A spouse (see footnote b)	$39	$52	$64	$77

70% - 100% without Children

Veteran Alone	$1,161	$1,349	$1,517	$2,527
Veteran with Spouse Only	$1,260	$1,462	$1,644	$2,669
Veteran with Spouse & One Parent	$1,339	$1,553	$1,746	$2,783
Veteran with Spouse and Two Parents	$1,418	$1,644	$1,848	$2,897
Veteran with One Parent	$1,240	$1,440	$1,619	$2,641
Veteran with Two Parents	$1,319	$1,531	$1,721	$2,755
Additional for A/A spouse (see footnote b)	$90	$103	$116	$129

30% - 60% with Children

Dependent Status	30%	40%	50%	60%
Veteran with Spouse & Child	$429	$610	$850	$1068
Veteran with Child Only	$384	$550	$776	$978
Veteran with Spouse, One Parent and Child	$463	$655	$907	$1136
Veteran with Spouse, Two Parents and Child	$497	$700	$964	$1,204
Veteran with One Parent and Child	$418	$595	$833	$1046
Veteran with Two Parents and Child	$452	$640	$890	$1114
Add for Each Additional Child Under Age 18	$21	$28	$35	$42
Each Additional Schoolchild Over Age 18 (see footnote a)	$68	$90	$113	$136
Additional for A/A spouse (see footnote b)	$39	$52	$64	$77

70% - 100% with Children

Veteran with Spouse & Child	$1,332	$1,545	$1,737	$2,772
Veteran with Child Only	$1,228	$1,425	$1,603	$2,623
Veteran with Spouse, One Parent and Child	$1,411	$1,636	$1,839	$2,886
Veteran with Spouse, Two Parents and Child	$1,490	$1,727	$1,941	$3,000
Veteran with One Parent and Child	$1,307	$1,516	$1,705	$2,737
Veteran with Two Parents and Child	$1,386	$1,607	$1,807	$2,851
Add for Each Additional Child Under Age 18	$49	$56	$63	$71
Each Additional Schoolchild Over Age 18 (see footnote a)	$158	$181	$204	$227
Additional for A/A spouse (see footnote b)	$90	$103	$116	$129

FOOTNOTES:

a. Rates for each school child are shown separately. They are not included with any other compensation rates. All other entries on this chart reflecting a rate for children show the rate payable for children under 18 or helpless. To find the amount payable to a 70% disabled veteran with a spouse and four children, one of whom is over 18 and attending school, take the 70% rate for a veteran with a spouse and 3 children, $1,430, and add the rate for one school child, $158. The total amount payable is $1,588.

b. Where the veteran has a spouse who is determined to require A/A, add the figure shown as "additional for A/A spouse" to the amount shown for the proper dependency code. For example, veteran has A/A spouse and 2 minor children and is 70% disabled. Add $90, additional for A/A spouse, to the rate for a 70% veteran with dependency code 12, $1,381. The total amount payable is $1,471.

Chapter 8
0% is good

In the previous chapter, I mentioned that seemingly a rating of a 0% is easier to be upgraded than receiving a rating of 10% or more. This means the VA has acknowledged your disability however, is refusing to take responsibility for causing or contributing to your disability. There is a clear case for plausible deniability. The VA knows under normal circumstances a person would not abuse their bodies in this way. Here is some more of the VA's doublespeak about your 0% rating:

Zero percent evaluations.

"In every instance where the schedule does not provide a zero percent evaluation for a diagnostic code, a zero percent evaluation shall be assigned when the requirements for a compensable evaluation are not met." **8**

By giving you a rating of 0%, you were able to challenge the system for an increase in your disability compensation. My suggestion is to wait until there's a change in your physical or mental status before seeking to a re-evaluation for each disability. Captain Smith left the army after her obligation was up. She applied for VA disability benefits and was upset when she received several ratings of 0% on her broken ankle and chronic fatigue syndrome. I explained to her that a 0% rating was a good thing. I suggested that she go consult with a non VA doctor about her ankle and her battle with chronic fatigue syndrome. Following my advice, she brought the paperwork back to the VA doctors where she then filed a re-evaluation of her claim. Within six months, her claim was processed and she received a 20% increase for both ailments. The key it is getting outside consultation on any injury, disease, illness or symptom. Second opinions will strengthen your claim and provide added weigh if you need to file an appeal. I would like to make this point. Keeping your paperwork straight and in order will prevent any slowdown or delay of the processing of your claim. You must remember that this system is broken and you must do everything possible to benefit you and your family.

Chapter 9
Appeal or not to appeal

"Appeal or not to appeal?" that is the question. Veterans are finding themselves ask this question every day. Due to the backlog of appeals in the system the average wait time just to get your appeal heard is over three to four years! The truth of the matter is appealing your VA claim decision you must have the stamina of a marathon runner because unfathomable and unbelievable wait times it takes just to have your appeal heard by the Board of Veterans' Appeals. This part of the process is often corrupted by poor process management. The Office of The Inspector General of the VA most frequently cited evidence that the quality of claim adjudication is inadequate and a high rate of appealed cases (90% of which are compensation cases) are remanded (sent back) by the board of veterans appeals to the originating VA regional office for additional information or reconsideration. Currently about half of all appealed cases are remanded - which can add an additional two years to the veterans point for a decision on their benefit claims. 9 This statement here drives my point home about the indifference of the VA. The high remand rate, combined with the Board of Veterans Appeals ruling in favor of veterans in 20% of the appealed cases plus another 10% of appeal cases reversed by their regional offices themselves on remand, is interpreted by veterans service organizations (which represents veterans before the Board of Veterans Appeals) as proof that the regional offices are not properly adjudicating veterans claims. 10

How does the appeal process work? A veteran who is dissatisfied with a decision may appeal first to the Board of Veterans Appeals (which may take up to three years to be heard) and then to the Court of Veterans Appeals (which may add another two to three years to the process). The Board of Veterans Appeals is a component of the VA that is responsible for deciding appeals of decisions made by the regional offices while the Court of Veterans Appeals is a separate judicial body which is responsible for deciding appeals of decisions made by the Board the Veterans Appeals. The VA has added a few more steps to confuse and delay the appeals process. Most veterans would give up and accept anything the VA would give them at this point. As mentioned in previous chapters, the VA knows this type of stall tactic will drive off all but the most determined veterans. So we're back at the beginning ... "***Appeal or not to appeal? This is the question***."

Instead of appealing your case, it is better to wait six months to one year and seek a re-evaluation of your claim. The re-evaluation process takes four months to eight months on average to be processed by the VA in most cases. During this time, you must make all your doctor's visits, and seek an outside opinion for your medical condition. This is imperative that you actively manage your disability benefits because the VA won't help you.

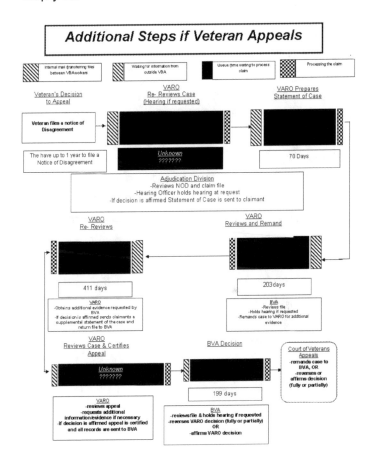

Looking at the diagram on the previous page, we see several questionable steps that the VA will take to delay, stall or deny a veteran's claim. In the real world, people get fired, businesses fail, or processes are changed if there are many unknowns or missed steps. However at the VA this behavior is rewarded and if not rewarded tolerated by the leadership at the VA. Think back on the nature of several of your business and personal relationships. Think about the times when you did not give a clear-cut answer and what were the consequences or ramifications of the lapsed of knowledge. Basically, you lost your credibility and was marked many full life as being incompetent or worthless. There is no excuse for the VA not to be able to give a clear-cut answer or indicate these processes take. You must pass yourself what is real cost beside wasted time and personal frustration. Now the system is overwhelmed and understaffed and the leaders in Congress and at the VA are dragging their feet to solve this dire problem. For more information about your VA benefits go to www.vaoutsider@bellsouth.net

Chapter 10
Oh by the way...

We have reached the end of this journey. I hope that you will follow these instructions, take my advise these and annotates to heart. The VA is trying to change I will give them that. However the change is very slowly and at the expense of veterans. This is a national disgrace that must be corrected at all costs. We must press our elected officials in the Senate and in the House of Representatives. In closing I have a list of "Oh by the ways!"

Oh by the ways...

- There is no rushing the VA to quickly process your claim

- Filing a congressional complaint against the VA sometimes it is counterproductive however it is necessary in the bigger scheme of things

- Keep copies of all of the documents that you provided the VA, the dates, times and names of the person(s) who you spoke to and type of treatment that you received from the VA

- The VA is an organization ran by people and you know people will take things personally.

So, if someone said is this not personal do not believe them

- Make all your appointments and be on time

- You must be responsible for your own claim ... this means you must manage your part of the process by having your paperwork in order and documentation clear and concise

- Talk to other veterans about the disability claims process

- Last but least you must be prepared fight for your rights in your disability compensation because the VA will not I repeat will not, give it to you without a struggle

End notes

1. Office of the Inspector General, <u>Summary Report on VA Claims Processing Issues, (Office of The Inspector General Washington, DC 1997) 15.</u>

2. Ibid 15 – 16

3. Ari Shapiro, <u>Army Blocks Disability Paperwork Aid at Fort Drum. (National Public Radio, 2008) 1.</u>

4. Ibid 1

5. Office of the Inspector General, <u>Summary Report on VA Claims Processing Issues, (Office of The Inspector General Washington, DC 1997) 30.</u>

6. Ibid 49 – 50

7. Title 38 – <u>Pensions, Bonuses, and Veterans' Relief (Chapter I – Department of Veterans Affairs Part -4 Subpart A- General Policy in Rating) 4.7</u>

8. Ibid 4.31

9. Office of the Inspector General, <u>Summary Report on VA Claims Processing Issues, (Office of The Inspector General Washington, DC 1997) 2.</u>

10. Ibid 2

Charts and Illustrations Sheet

1. Information Provided by the VA Representative: Provided by Veterans Resource Group, 2007

2. Does Cronyism and Nepotism Run Rampant within the VA: Provided by Veterans Resource Group, 2007

3. Illustration 1: VA Form 21-526, Part B – Compensation, 2006

4. Illustration 2: VA Form 21-4138 – Statement In Support of Claim, 2007

5. VA's Customer Care Rating by Veterans: Provided by Veterans Resource Group, 2007

6. Chart of Claims Adjudication/Appeals Process (Typical Original Compensation Claims) Office of The Inspector General Appendix IV, 2007 pg 93

7. Illustration 3: VA Form 21-4138 – Statement In Support of Claim, 2007

8. VA Compensation and Pension Payment Rates Department of Veterans Affairs Effective, 2007

9. Chart of Claims Adjudication/Appeals Process (Additional Steps if Veterans Appeals) Office of The Inspector General Appendix IV, 2007 pg 94, 2007

Work Cited List

1. Department of Veterans Affair. Office of the Inspector General. Summary Report on VA Claims Processing Issues. Washington, DC, 1997.

2. Shapiro, Ari. "The Army Blocks Disability Paperwork Aid at Fort Drum." National Public Radio, 2008 Morning Edition page 2.

3. Shapiro, Ari. "The Army Blocks Disability Paperwork Aid at Fort Drum." National Public Radio, 2008 Morning Edition page 1.

4. United States. Code of Federal Regulations. Title 38: Pensions, Bonuses and Veterans' Relief. Department of Veterans Affairs. 4 Subpart A – General Policy in Rating.

Web sites you should know

www.va.gov – US Department of Veterans Affairs

www.woundedwarriors.org – The Wounded Warriors Project

www.nmfa.org – National Military Families Association

www.fisherhouse.org – The Fisher House

www.vawatchdog.org - The VA Watchdog

www.military.com – Military.com

www.nchv.org – The National Coalition for Homeless Veterans

www.veteransassistance.org – Veterans Assistance Foundation

List of forms

Form Numbers	Form Titles
VBA 21-0501	Veterans Benefits Timetable Information for Veterans Recently Separated from Active Military Service
VBA 21-526 A,B,C and D	Veterans Application for Compensation And/Or Pension
VBA 21-4138	Statement in Support of Claim
VBA 21-22	Appointment of Veterans Service Organization as Claimant's Representation
VBA 21-4142	Authorization and Consent to Release Information to the Department of Veterans Affairs
VBA 21-0506	Notice of Your Due Process Rights
VBA 21-8940	Veteran's Application For Increased Compensation Based on Unemployability
VBA 21-0781	Statement in Support of Claim for Service Connection For Post Traumatic Stress Disorder (PTSD)
VBA 22-5490	Application For Survivor's and Dependents' Educational Assistance